MW01622516

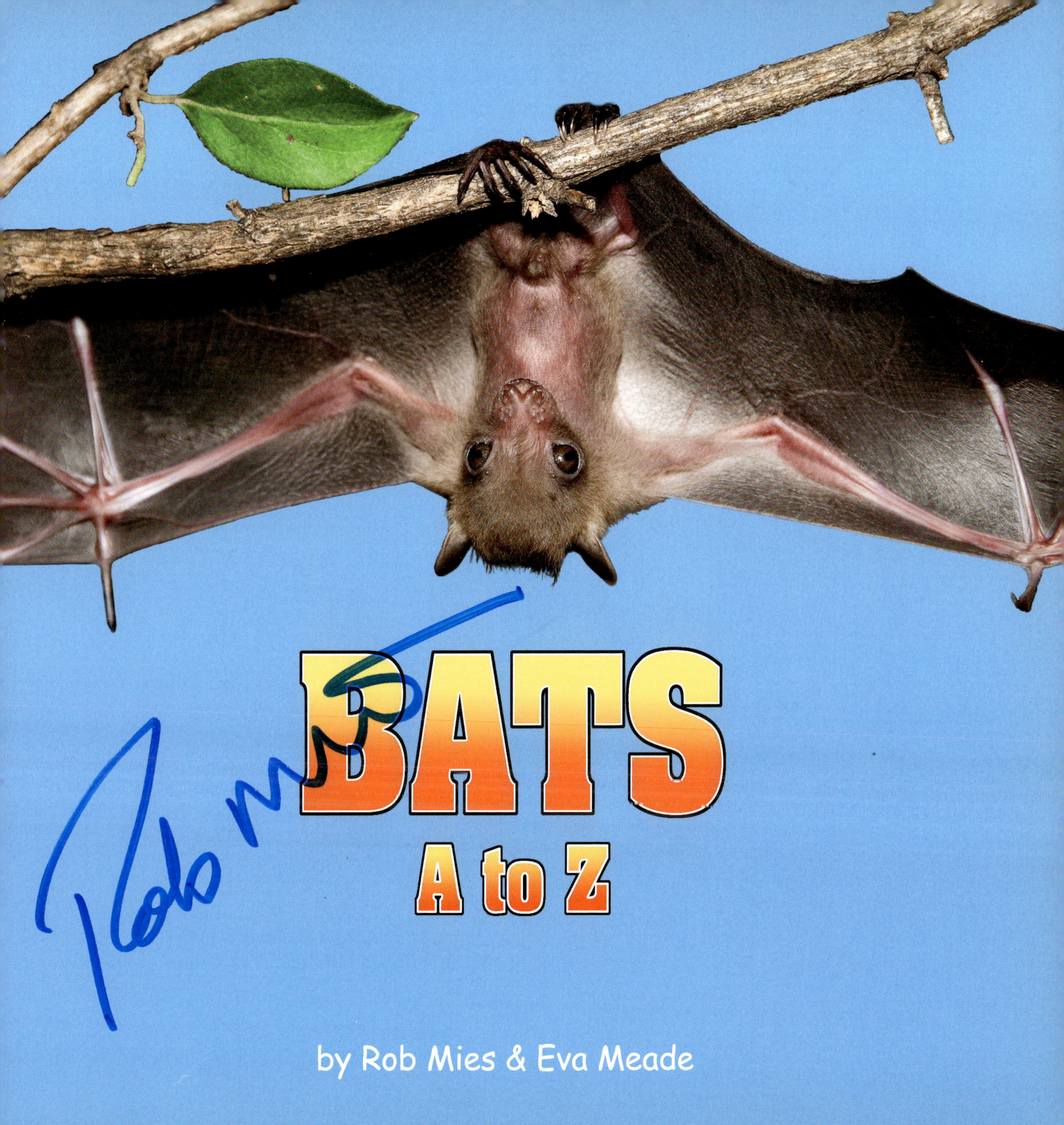

BATS
A to Z

by Rob Mies & Eva Meade

ACKNOWLEDGEMENTS

We would like to thank the following for all their help and encouragement:
Karen McDiarmid without whose patience and positive encouragement this book would not have been completed and to our loving kids (Georgia, Madison, and Andrew)
who endured 3 years of looking at the book taped to our living room walls.

This book features an amazing selection of photographs.
We are so thankful for the use of these images from the following terrific photographers:
©www.SteveGettle.com, ©Doug Locke, Tim Carter, David Redell, Dick Wilkins, George Smiley, Ruth Vrbensky, Dawn Vezina, Betty Murcko, Kerri Morgan, Bernal Rodriguez-Herrera, Gerry Carter, Frank Cloud, Nickolay Hristov, Louise Allen, Fiona Reid, Carol Hunt, and MetroParent.com

Inquiries about this book should be addressed to:

Mies & Meade Publishing
Bloomfield Hills, Michigan • info@robmies.com
www.robmies.com

A portion of the proceeds support the care and feeding of the many rescued bats, educational programming, and collaborative wildlife preservation projects at the Organization for Bat Conservation.
www.batconservation.org

Mies, Rob & Meade, Eva
Bats, A to Z

by Rob Mies & Eva Meade

Photographs by Allen, Louise; Carter, Gerry; Carter, Tim; Cloud, Frank; Gettle, Steve; Hristov, Nickolay; Hunt, Carol; Locke, Doug; MetroParent.com; Morgan, Kerri; Murcko, Betty; Redell, David; Reid, Fiona; Rodriguez-Herrera, Bernal; Smiley, George; Venzina, Dawn; Vrbensky, Ruth; Wilkins, Dick

Summary: Fun facts about bats and an amazing collection of photographs educate and engage the reader regardless of age.

Book design by Karen McDiarmid.
Color expertise by Greg Dunn of Digital Imagery.
Additional artwork by Eva Meade.

Printed and bound August 2013 — #86943
Friesens of Altona, Manitoba, Canada

ISBN 978-0-9833875-0-3
1. Bats — Juvenile Literature
2. Alphabet — Juvenile Literature

Library of Congress Control Number: 2013913293

10 9 8 7 6 5 4 3 2 1

THIS BOOK IS DEDICATED TO BATS AROUND THE WORLD FOR THE IMPORTANT PART THEY PLAY IN THE ECOSYSTEM AND TO ALL THE PEOPLE WHO WORK TIRELESSLY TO PROTECT THEM FROM EXTINCTION.

Rob Mies is an exciting and adventurous scientist, conservationist, TV personality, and bat expert who has focused his passion toward educating and entertaining people about one of the most unique and misunderstood animals in the world. His energetic, charismatic, and captivating personality leads to countless speaking engagements and sold-out audiences. This author, Executive Director, and Founder of the Organization for Bat Conservation has appeared on many television shows with his furry, winged friends including The Tonight Show, The Ellen DeGeneres Show, The Today Show, Live with Regis and Kelly, Late Night with Conan O'Brien, Fox & Friends, and Martha Stewart.

Eva Meade, an entrepreneur with a degree in fine art and photography, has worked many years in design and creative consulting. She donates much of her time to the protection of animals, raising awareness about animal cruelty, and educating people about wildlife conservation. She and Rob live in Bloomfield Hills, Michigan with their three children and rescued golden-doodle named "Mac."

Aa

ASIA

NORTH AMERICA

AFRICA

AUSTRALIA

SOUTH AMERICA

From AFRICA to AUSTRALIA,
ASIA to AMERICA,
ALASKA to ALABAMA
bats are found all over the world,
except in extremely hot deserts
and cold polar regions
like ANTARCTICA.

ALBINO bats are rare.

Can you find the ALBINO bat in the picture?

AMAZING ACROBATS!

Don't you wish you could fly like a bat?

Bats are **AWESOME ANIMALS!**
They are the only mammals that can fly!

They can twist and turn to dart after their prey.

Bb
BATS are BENEFICIAL. They pollinate flowers, spread seeds, and eat lots of BUGS.
BATS are great moms.
Once a year, moms have one or two BABIES.
BABY BATS are called pups.
BABIES drink mom's milk.
I love you mommy!
BABY Egyptian fruit bat

They call me a **BIG BROWN BAT** but my wingspan is only 13 inches.

The North American **BIG BROWN BAT** eats 1000s of crop-damaging **BEETLES** each night.

The endangered **BUMBLEBEE BAT** from Thailand, weighing only 2 grams, may be the world's smallest mammal.

Moms teach **BABIES** to fly, catch food, avoid predators and show them where to hibernate or migrate by watching.

Newborns cling under mom's wing, even when she flies.

Cc
Many types of bats like to live in CAVES for protection from weather and predators.
Bats are so COOL!
Look how the COLONY of bats hangs from the CEILING of this CAVE!
Some bats are CARNIVORES. They eat insects, fish, frogs, birds, lizards, scorpions, mice, and even other bats.

The thin wing skin feels like your eyelid.
Thumbs up, dude!
CAMOUFLAGE keeps bats safe from predators.
Thumb
5th Finger
2nd Finger
4th Finger
3rd Finger
Bats are in their own scientific group called CHIROPTERA (ki-rop-ter-a), which means "Hand Wing."

All over the world, bats are in **DANGER**.

DAMAGING pesticides sprayed on crops in fields kill the insects that bats eat.

DEFORESTATION causes habitat loss since trees are home for many bats.

A **DISEASE** called White-Nose Syndrome has killed millions of bats and is spreading quickly.

As Bats Fly they

DIP

DIVE

DART

Chasing their Prey

Bats come out after **DARK**. There are fewer predators, more insects and less competitors (like birds) for food.

There is great DIVERSITY in bats around the world. There are over 1,100 kinds.
Body sizes range from 2 inches to 33 inches long!
Wingspans range from 6 inches to 6 feet!
There are many DIFFERENT colored bats from white to black, solid colored, spotted, and even striped!
DOG-FACED bat
Do you have friends that are DIFFERENT than you?

Ee

Bats are important to the **ENVIRONMENT** and the **ECONOMY**. They pollinate plants, spread seeds and **EAT** garden pests.

Do you think I'm **EATING** an avocado, banana, fig or mango? I like them all!

Bats are not blind. Their **EYES** work like ours, some 3 times better!

Bats **EAT EVERYTHING** from insects and fruits to nectar, fish, small mammals, amphibians and even blood!

Some bats are **ENDANGERED** (almost **EXTINCT**) because of forest destruction, human fear, pollution, pesticides and climate change.

Bats have many **ENEMIES**. Owls, hawks, snakes and raccoons like to **EAT** bats!

Insect-eating bats make high-pitched sounds called **ECHOLOCATION**. The ultrasonic sounds come out of their mouth or nose, hit an object, and bounce back to the bat's ears.

Bats **EARS** funnel the sounds of their babies, **ECHOLOCATION** and predators.

Ff
FUNNY FACES

"Say Cheese!"

"Delicioso!"

"Check out my ears!"

"Ha Ha Ha!"

FANTASTIC FLYERS

I can FLY 20 to 50 MPH! What FUN!

The oldest bat FOSSIL is from Wyoming and dates back over 50 million years.

FISHING bats echolocate to find a FISH or ripple in water, then swoop down to grab a meal.

This FURRY FRUIT-EATER is called a FLYING FOX because of her FOX-LIKE FACE.

FRUIT bats chew on FRUIT, suck out the juice, and spit out the pulp.

Gg

The **GIANT** of the bat world is the Malayan flying fox. It's about the size of a Canada **GOOSE**.

The largest bats are found in southeast Asia, including Malaysia and India.

Insect-eating bats eat **GARDEN** pests like **GRASSHOPPERS**.

Bats are very clean animals. Like cats, they spend a lot of time **GROOMING** themselves and their babies.

Aren't you **GLAD** you don't **GROOM** with your tongue?

Bat **HOUSES** give bats a safe place to sleep and care for their young.

A bat **HOUSE** should be:

- Painted a dark color
- At least 15 feet **HIGH**
- Facing the sun
- In a clearing
- On a pole or side of a building

HOARY bats are the most widespread in the United States and the first land mammal on the **HAWAIIAN** Islands, before **HUMANS!**

Zzzzzzz

Some bats **HIBERNATE** (sleep) through the long, cold winter. Instead of eating, they use stored fat for energy.

The **HABITAT** of bats varies greatly. From dry deserts to tropical rainforests and even snowy regions, bats are found almost everywhere! Many bats choose **HOLLOW** trees, rock crevices, under tree bark and caves to call **HOME.**

About 70% of bats eat night-flying INSECTS like beetles, moths, flies and mosquitoes.

The largest group of bats in the world — 20 million Mexican free-tail bats — lives in Texas. They eat up to a half million pounds of INSECTS in one summer night.

A pregnant female bat can eat up to half her body weight in INSECTS each night. That's like you eating 20 large pizzas every day!

Bats learn to fly by **IMITATING** their moms, just like humans learn to walk by watching other people.

Are bats **INTELLIGENT?** Many scientists think so!

In zoos, bats have been taught to open their wings on command, crawl to a certain place when told, and come when their name is called.

Jj

This JAMAICAN fruit bat is found in Central and South America. It is also called a "leaf-nosed" bat because its nose resembles a leaf.

Most bats are found in the JUNGLES near the equator. The warm and humid climate allows for amazing bat species diversity.

Most bats cannot take flight from the ground, but a few bats (like the vampire) can JUMP up to 6 times their height!

JUMP!

JUMP!

How high can you JUMP?

Kk

Mammoth Cave in KENTUCKY, is the longest cave in the world. There are 6 different KINDS of bats that live in this cave.

There are many KINDS of bats in the world.

WHITE BATS
SPOTTED BATS
RED BATS
YELLOW BATS
TINY BATS
GIANT BATS
FLUFFY HAIR BATS
NAKED-BACKED BATS
SHORT HAIR BATS
BROWN BATS

KUDOS to Park Rangers working to restore the cave's ecology!

KEEP a safe distance from bats. They are wild animals. Bats will not attack, but will bite to protect themselves.

L1
The LIFESPAN of most bats is about 17 years, but the oldest bat found was 41.
Bugs may be pests to you, but are LUNCH to me!
The LITTLE brown bat, one of the most common bats in North America, LIVES up to 30 years old in the wild. During warm months it is an important predator of garden pests while half the year they hibernate in a cave.

LONG-tongued bats are small, delicate bats with long narrow muzzles.

They can hover like a hummingbird drinking nectar from flowers.

The tube-**LIPPED** nectar bat of Ecuador can stretch its tongue more than 1-1/2 times the **LENGTH** of its body.

How **LONG** can you stick out your tongue?

All bats with noses shaped like **LEAVES** are commonly called **LEAF**-nosed bats.

Some **LEAF**-nosed bats eat insects. Others eat fruit, nectar, pollen, frogs, birds, other bats, and even blood!

By echolocating out of their nose, **LEAF**-nosed bats can fly with food in their mouths and not run into things or get caught by predators. Folds of skin around their nostrils help direct sound waves.

Mm

MEGABAT

LARGE BATS

LARGE EYES

SMALLER EARS

FOX-LIKE FACES

Found only in Africa, southeast Asia, and Australia

Eats flowers, pollen, leaves and especially fruit and nectar

Does not use echolocation but relies on keen eyesight, hearing and sense of smell

I'm a MAGNIFICENT MEGABAT!

Fact: Bats are more afraid of you than you are of them.

MYTH: Bats are blind.
Fact: Some bats see better than humans.

MYTH: Bats are MICE.
Fact: Bats are MAMMALS but more like primates.

MYTH: Bats make nests in hair.
Fact: No, bats prefer trees or caves.

MICROBAT

SMALL BATS

SMALL EYES

LARGE EARS

MEGABATS and **MICROBATS** are the 2 types of bats.

Found on every continent except Antarctica

Eats insects, fruit, nectar, fish, frogs, birds, blood, and even other bats

Uses echolocation to find food and navigate the night

Some bats **MIGRATE** more than 1,000 miles! WOW!

After consuming **MOTHS** all summer, 20 **MILLION MEXICAN** free-tail bats **MIGRATE** from Bracken Cave, Texas to **MEXICO**.

Nn
Bats are NOCTURNAL
(active at NIGHT and asleep during the day).
NOCTURNAL animals have highly developed
senses of hearing and smell, and specially
adapted eyesight. They usually have large
eyes, large ears, long whiskers,
and use echolocation.
Check out
this bat
in flight!

Leaf-NOSE bats can echolocate while they fly with fruit in their mouths.

NECTAR-feeding bats have long, pointed NOSES that fit just right into flowers.

The vampire bat's NOSE is flat against its head so it can get close to its prey.

Flying foxes' NOSES are like a dog's muzzle that helps smell ripe fruit.

Over 150 rescued bats live at **O.B.C.**, including bats that eat fruit, insects, and even blood.

The bats that live at **O.B.C.** are given toys to help their mind and body by discovering new things.

ORANGES are OUTSTANDING!

Inspiring people to actively conserve bats.

People come to O.B.C. from around the world to see these OUTSTANDING nocturnal animals up close.

Saving bat habitat around the world.

OBC

ORGANIZATION FOR

BATCONSERVATION

Supporting scientists that study bats.

The animals that live at O.B.C. travel across the United States helping teach OTHERS about bats.

OOOO this flower smells delicious!

Learn more about us at www.batconservation.org.

Pp

From **PHILADELPHIA** to **PANAMA** to **PAPUA NEW GUINEA**, the benefits of bats are great.

They are the main **PREDATORS** of flying insects at night. Some **POLLINATE** flowers.

However, there are fewer bats around today.

Wonder what you can do to **PROTECT** bats?

PUT up a bat house!

Recycle and reduce waste, clean up litter, and turn off electronics in your home.

Teach your friends and family that bats are really great for the environment.

PLANT a wildflower garden!

Flowers like evening **PRIMROSE** attract bugs that bats eat.

Allow fragrant **PERENNIAL** vines to climb walls or fences. They **PROVIDE** roosting sites.

Bats will be **PLEASED** if you garden organically; **PESTICIDES** are very harmful to bats.

The **PALLID** bat is found in desert climates of western North America.

Its **PALE,** yellow-brown color helps it hide from **PREDATORS** by blending into the rocky background. Some of their favorite foods include grasshoppers, crickets and scorpions.

In the rainforests of north **QUEENSLAND, AUSTRALIA,** there are many kinds of flying fox bats. During the day, these giant fruit bats live in large groups at the top of sunny rainforest trees. At dusk, they fly off in search of sweet fruit.

Bats are so lightweight, they're nearly silent flyers.

Can you run aroun as QUIETL as I fly?

Bats can fly very **QUIETLY** using their wings like a swimmer doing the butterfly stroke. Wings are made of two layers of thin skin stretched over small, lightweight bones. It's so thin you can see blood moving through the blood vessels.

Bats can eat a large **QUANTITY** of food.

This African straw-colored fruit bat can eat up to 2-1/2 times its weight in fruit each night.

One North American little brown bat can eat several thousand insects each night.

Bats need large **QUANTITIES** of food to produce enough energ to be the only flying mammal.

The place where bats live is called their **ROOST**.

Many bats like to **ROOST** inside a tree, cave, building, or under a bridge.

Many bats live in attics, barns, and bat houses. Some bats live together and others live by themselves.

Welcome to our ROOST!

What does your home look like?

RED bats like to live alone hanging by one foot in a live tree. This helps them keep warm and stay hidden from predators.

They may bite to defend themselves. Most are healthy and live a long time. **RARELY,** they get a disease called **RABIES** that can be spread to other mammals. If bitten, wash your hands and see a doctor.

Ss

STRAW-
Colored
Fruit Bat

Weighs almost one pound!

3-foot wing-span!

Hangs out with lots of friends!

STRAW-colored fruit bats are one of the largest bats in Africa. These very SOCIAL bats roost in tall trees during the day, where they are often noisy and restless.

The largest fruit bat colony in the world is a group of 8 million STRAW-colored fruit bats that live in Kasanka National Park in Zambia, Africa.

SEEDS that aren't digested are dispersed from this end throughout rainforests while bats fly.

I have SUPER SPOTS!

The SPOTTED bat looks like a Dalmatian with white SPOTS on its black furry back.

Are bats STRANGE looking?

YES! Some are, to us!

Do you think YOU are...

...STRANGE looking to bats?

The SPEAR-nosed bat's long horn-like nose is used to echolocate while flying with food in its mouth.

The SUCKER-footed bat has round STICKY pads on wrists and elbows so it can roost inside unfurled tropical leaves.

Wrinkled-faced bats, SLIT-faced bats, and naked-backed bats are some other STRANGE looking bats!

Tt

The Baobab TREE is called the "TREE of Life" because it is home to many animals.

Big fruit bats live at the TOPS of giant rainforest TREES.

Under bark of dead and dying TREES live small insect-eating bats.

Vampire bats find shelter inside hollow TREES.

Bats use their TONGUE to drink nectar, clean their fur, smash fruit, and drink water in flight.

They use their THUMB for climbing, grooming, holding fruit, and defending against a roost-mate who wants to steal their meal.

Most bats have a TAIL.

Some have skin between their legs that connects to the tail. This TAIL membrane acts like another wing, helping them take-off.

TAILS are also used to catch insects, slow flight, and cradle a newborn baby.

There are also mouse-tailed bats, free-tailed bats, short-tailed bats, and bats that have no TAILS.

TENT-making bats camp out in TENTS made of leaves.

TENT-making bats chew on the veins of a leaf to build their home which resembles a turned over boat.

Their TENT shades them from hot TROPICAL sun, heavy rains, and predators.

This TENT-making bat is perched on a researcher's THUMB.

Bats are the primary insect-eating predators of night-time. Scientists estimate that bats save U.S. farmers over $4 billion annually in insect control.

Some bats of the UNITED STATES.

Silver-haired Bat

Western Red Bat

Hoary Bat

Western Yellow Bat

There are about 50 different species of bats in the UNITED STATES.
Little Brown Bat
Big Brown Bat
Indiana Bat
Rafinesque's Big-eared Bat
Mexican Long-tongued Bat

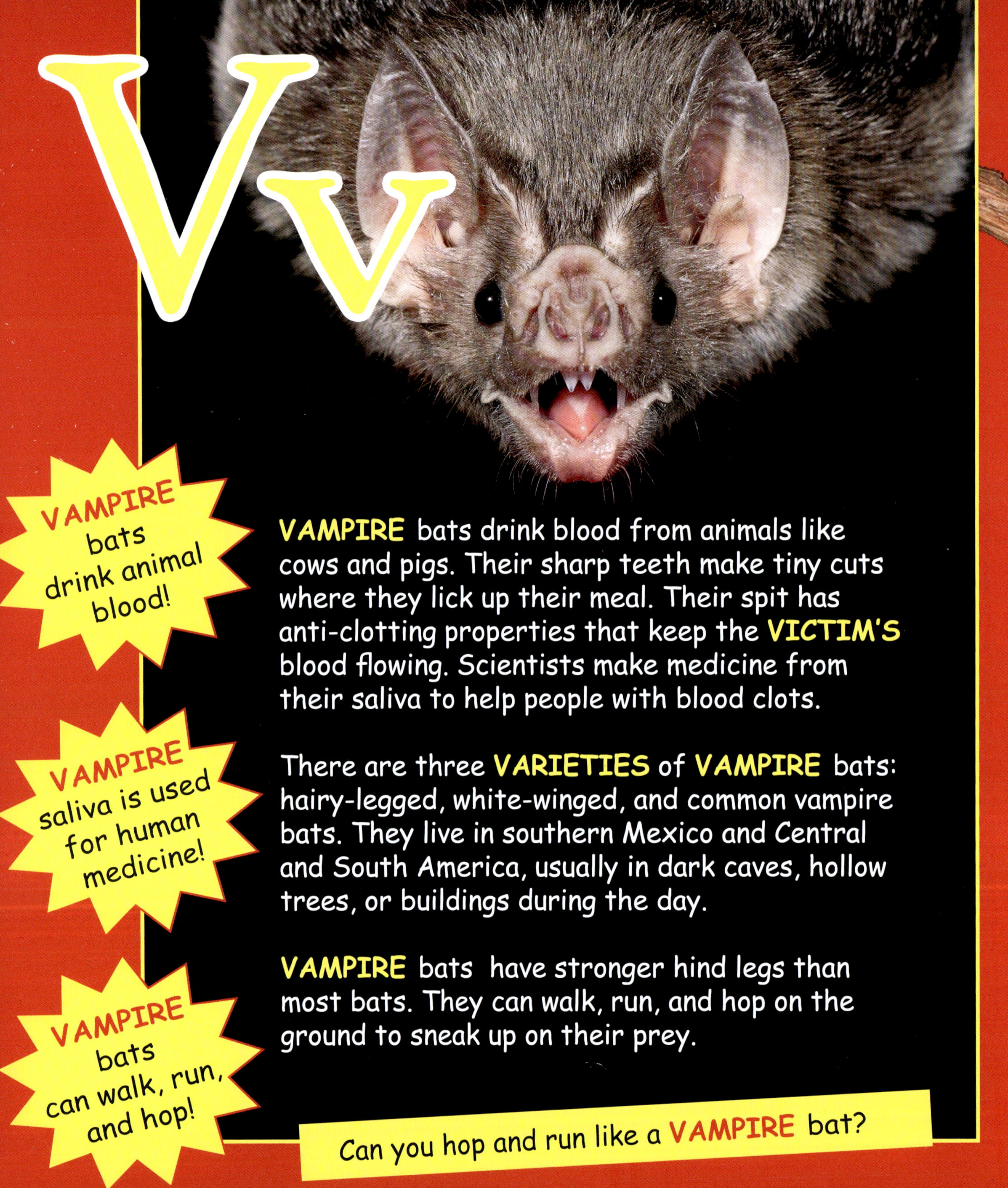

Vv

VAMPIRE bats drink animal blood!

VAMPIRE saliva is used for human medicine!

VAMPIRE bats can walk, run, and hop!

VAMPIRE bats drink blood from animals like cows and pigs. Their sharp teeth make tiny cuts where they lick up their meal. Their spit has anti-clotting properties that keep the **VICTIM'S** blood flowing. Scientists make medicine from their saliva to help people with blood clots.

There are three **VARIETIES** of **VAMPIRE** bats: hairy-legged, white-winged, and common vampire bats. They live in southern Mexico and Central and South America, usually in dark caves, hollow trees, or buildings during the day.

VAMPIRE bats have stronger hind legs than most bats. They can walk, run, and hop on the ground to sneak up on their prey.

Can you hop and run like a **VAMPIRE** bat?

Bats are **VULNERABLE** to changes in the environment. When forests are cut down, rivers are polluted, or chemicals are sprayed it is harmful to bats.

Flying fox bats use excellent color **VISION** instead of echolocation. All bats can see, but Megabats use their large eyes to navigate the night, find food, and watch for predators.

Bats are the only mammals with WINGS.

Some are long and narrow, others are short and broad.

A bat WING has:

- A thumb
- 4 long fingers
- An upper arm
- A forearm
- Thin skin that stretches across the bones and connects to the sides of the body and hind legs.

Look closely! Can you find the parts of this bat's WINGS?

WEIRD and WONDERFUL facts about bats!

The smallest bat, the bumblebee bat, WEIGHS about as much as a dime with a WINGSPAN of 6 inches!

The largest bat, the Malayan flying fox, WEIGHS up to 2 pounds with a WINGSPAN of 6 feet.

WRINKLE-faced bats have extra long skin around their chin that can be pulled up over their face to camouflage themselves as they sleep in live trees.

Not so WONDERFUL facts about bats

WIND farms produce cleaner energy but can be harmful to bats while they migrate.

Many bats WRAP their wings around themselves to hide from predators.

Want to see a bat in the WILD?

Take a bat WALK! Bats search for insects just after sunset.

Look for them near streetlights, WATER, and the edge of WOODS.

During the day, identify habitat like dead trees, rock crevices, old buildings, and evergreen trees.

WHITE-Nose Syndrome is a fungus that grows on bats hibernating in cold caves in the WINTER.

The fungus WAKES the bats and WASTES their energy. They fly out to feed on insects but, in WINTER, there are none.

Bats need WETLANDS. Dead trees are great homes to some bats.

Bats drink WATER in flight, skimming over ponds, lakes, or rivers with their mouths open.

Xx

The skeleton of a bat can be seen when a veterinarian takes an **X-RAY** picture. We can see how the wing of the bat looks like a hand, with four long fingers and one small thumb. Have you ever had an **X-RAY** taken?

Bats come in many different colors including red, white, and YELLOW.

The North American YELLOW bat is an insect-eater that lives alone. They like to hang in Spanish moss that grows in trees.

Most bats have one or two babies each spring. YELLOW bats have up to four babies at a time!

How old are YOU?

Most bats live to be 15 to 20 YEARS old, but some bats have been found that are more than 40 YEARS old!

Zz

I never glide like a bird!

Do you ever see bats ZIPPING around?

My wings keep moving when I fly!

ZIG! ZAG!

ZOOM!

Many people think they see a bird when they actually see a bat. Bats ZIGZAG through the air. Birds usually fly straight.

One of the best places to see bats up close is at a ZOO. Most bats at ZOOS are tropical fruit bats. They are kept in hot, humid conditions like a tropical rainforest.